Ladybird  Readers

Hungry Animals

Series Editor: Sorrel Pitts
Written by Hazel Geatches

LADYBIRD BOOKS

UK | USA | Canada | Ireland | Australia
India | New Zealand | South Africa

Ladybird Books is part of the Penguin Random House group of companies
whose addresses can be found at global.penguinrandomhouse.com.
www.penguin.co.uk   www.puffin.co.uk   www.ladybird.co.uk

First published by Ladybird Books, 2017
003

Printed in China

A CIP catalogue record for this book is available from the British Library

ISBN: 978-0-241-29844-2

All correspondence to:
Ladybird Books
Penguin Random House Children's
One Embassy Gardens, 8 Viaduct Gardens, London SW11 7BW

MIX
Paper from
responsible sources
FSC® C018179

Ladybird Readers

BBC earth

Hungry Animals

Inspired by BBC Earth TV series and
developed with input from BBC Earth
natural history specialists.

Contents

Picture words

cheetah

hummingbird

archerfish

eagle

beak

wing

insect

talon

Animals need food

All animals need food.

Some animals eat other animals. Some animals get food from plants.

Do you know what these animals eat?

cheetah

hummingbird

archerfish

eagle

Cheetahs

Cheetahs are big cats. They can run very fast, and they can see very well.

They use
their strong
teeth to
eat meat.

strong
teeth

How a cheetah gets food

A cheetah finds an animal. The cheetah stays very quiet in the grass, and watches the animal.

Then, it runs very fast.

The cheetah catches the animal, and eats it.

Hummingbirds

Hummingbirds are very small birds. They have long beaks.

Their food comes from flowers.

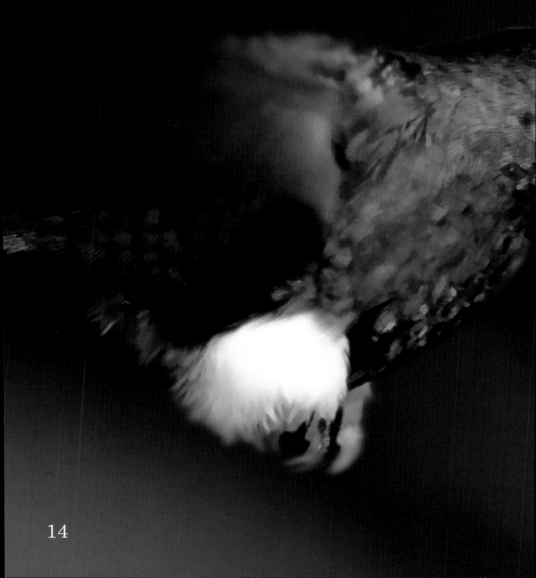

beak

How a hummingbird gets food

A hummingbird flies to a flower. It moves its wings very fast, and stays near the flower.

Then, it drinks the food from the flower.

Hummingbirds are always hungry.
They have lots of small drinks every day!

Archerfish

Some archerfish live in rivers. These fish can see very well.

They eat insects and other small animals.

How an archerfish gets food

An archerfish sees an insect above the water. Then, it hits the insect with water from its mouth.

archerfish

insect

The insect goes into the river, and the archerfish eats it.

Eagles

Eagles are very big birds. They have big wings and strong talons. They can see very well.

They eat small animals with their big beaks.

wing

talon

beak

23

How an eagle gets food

An eagle flies to find an animal.

Then, it flies down and catches the animal with its strong talons.

This eagle
lives near a river.
It eats fish.

Hungry animals

Animals are often
hungry because it is
not easy to find food.

This cheetah is running fast,
but it cannot catch the birds.

Many hummingbirds want food
from the same flowers.

One eagle has some food, but
the other eagle wants it.

Activities

The key below describes the skills practiced in each activity.

Spelling and writing

Reading

Speaking

Critical thinking

Preparation for the Cambridge Young Learners Exams

1 Look and read. Write *yes* or *no*.

Picture words

cheetah

hummingbird

beak

wing

archerfish

eagle

insect

talon

6

7

1 Are cheetahs big? ......yes......

2 Are hummingbirds small? ....

3 Do archerfish fly? ....

4 Have eagles got talons? ....

5 Have eagles and
hummingbirds got wings? ....

2 **Look and read. Write _All_ or _Some_.**

Animals need food

All animals need food.

Some animals eat other animals. Some animals get food from plants.

Do you know what these animals eat?

cheetah

8

hummingbird

archerfish

eagle

9

1 .... All .... animals need food.

2 .... animals eat other animals.

3 .... animals get food from plants.

4 .... eagles and hummingbirds eat with their beaks.

5 .... cheetahs have got four legs.

30

3 **Read the questions. Write the answers.** 📖 ✏️

Cheetahs

Cheetahs are big cats. They can run very fast, and they can see very well.

They use their strong teeth to eat meat.

strong teeth

1 Which animals are big cats?

　　Cheetahs are big cats.

2 Can cheetahs run fast?

　Yes, ...

3 Can cheetahs see well?

　Yes, ...

4 What do cheetahs eat?

　They eat ....

4 Look and read. Put a or a in the boxes.

How a cheetah gets food

A cheetah finds an animal. The cheetah stays very quiet in the grass, and watches the animal.

Then, it runs very fast.

The cheetah catches the animal, and eats it.

13

1 A cheetah finds an animal.

2 The cheetah is very quiet.

3 The animal watches the cheetah.

4 Then, the cheetah does not run.

5 **Work with a friend. Ask and answer questions about the pictures.**

1

What does the cheetah see?

The cheetah sees an animal.

2 What does the cheetah do?

3 What does the other animal do?

4 How fast does the cheetah run?

5 Does the cheetah catch the animal?

6 **Look at the letters.**
Write the words.

1 [H u b m i m i r n d s g]

H u m m i n g b i r d s
are very small birds.

2 [k e b a s]

They have long ....

3 [o o d f]

Their .... comes
from flowers.

4 [s i w n g]

A hummingbird flies
to a flower and moves
its .... very fast.

34

7 Look and read. Write the correct words on the lines. 📖 ✏️ ⭐

How a hummingbird gets food

A hummingbird flies to a flower. It moves its wings very fast, and stays near the flower.

Then, it drinks the food from the flower.

16

Hummingbirds are always hungry. They have lots of small drinks every day!

17

---

are   drinks   flies   moves   stays

---

1 Hummingbirds .... *are* .... always hungry.

2 A hummingbird .... to a flower.

3 It .... its wings very fast.

4 It .... near the flower.

5 Then, it .... the food from the flower.

8 Circle the correct words.

Archerfish

Some archerfish live in rivers. These fish can see very well.

They eat insects and other small animals.

How an archerfish gets food

An archerfish sees an insect above the water. Then, it hits the insect with water from its mouth.

insect

archerfish

The insect goes into the river, and the archerfish eats it.

1 Some archerfish live in **rivers.** / **gardens.**

2 Archerfish can **fly** / **see** very well.

3 They eat **flowers.** / **insects.**

4 The insect goes into the river, and the archerfish **eats** / **drinks** it.

How an archerfish gets food

An archerfish sees an insect above the water. Then, it hits the insect with water from its mouth.

insect

archerfish

20

The insect goes into the river, and the archerfish eats it.

21

.... The insect goes into the river.

_____1_____ The archerfish is hungry.

.... The archerfish eats the insect.

.... The archerfish hits the insect with water from its mouth.

.... The archerfish sees an insect above the water.

10 **Find the words.**

e	w	i	n	g	b	s	l
t	a	l	o	n	e	b	n
w	i	h	r	g	a	d	s
a	t	u	l	i	k	c	e
b	e	a	t	e	s	h	c
e	a	g	l	e	t	v	t

wing

eagle

talon

beak

1 Are eagles very big birds?

   a Yes, it is.

   b Yes, they are.

2 What do eagles eat?

   a They eats small animals.

   b They eat small animals.

3 Can eagles see very well?

   a Yes, they see.

   b Yes, they can.

4 Are their talons strong?

   a Yes, they do.

   b Yes, they are.

12 **Read the sentences and match them with the correct animals. Write 1—4.**

1 This animal can run very fast.

2 This animal lives in a river and it eats insects.

3 This animal is always hungry.

4 This animal has got strong talons.

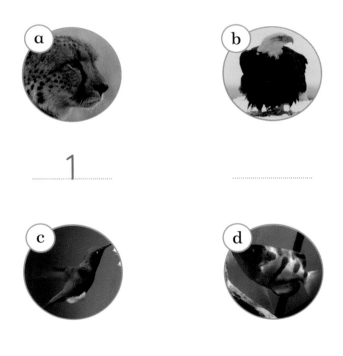

1

13 Circle the correct pictures.

1 Birds can fly because they have two of these.

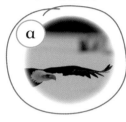 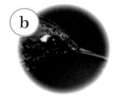

a   b

2 Eagles eat small animals with this.

a   b

3 This is food for the archerfish.

 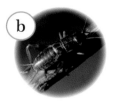

a   b

4 This small animal can move its wings very fast.

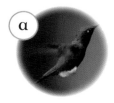 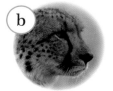

a   b

14 Write *big*, *small*, *long*, or *strong*.

1  The eagle is
a _____ big _____ bird.

2  It catches small animals with
its _____ talons.

3  The hummingbird is
a _____ bird.

4  It has a
_____ beak.

5  The cheetah eats animals
with its _____ teeth.

15 Write the missing letters.

ee   ea

1    e a t

2    m ____ ____ t

3    c h ____ ____ t a h

4    t ____ ____ t h

5    ____ ____ g l e

16 **Write the sentences.** 📖 ✏️

1 (eat) (from) (meat) (animals) (.) (Cheetahs)

Cheetahs eat meat
from animals.

2 (birds) (are) (Eagles) (big) (very) (.)

3 (always) (.) (Hummingbirds) (hungry) (are)

4 (drinks) (Hummingbirds) (every)
(have) (.) (day) (of) (lots)

17 **Match the two parts of the sentences.**

1 Cheetahs can run very fast, and

2 Archerfish can see

3 Eagles

4 Sometimes a cheetah runs fast, but

5 Animals are often hungry because

a fly to find food.

b it is not easy to find food.

c it cannot catch the animal.

d they can see very well.

e insects above the water.

18 **Work with a friend. Ask and answer questions about hungry animals.**

1 *What do cheetahs eat?*

They eat meat from other animals.

2 Where do hummingbirds find food?

3 What do archerfish eat?

4 Why are animals often hungry?

19 Write *T* (true) or *F* (false).

Hungry animals

Animals are often hungry because it is not easy to find food.

Many hummingbirds want food from the same flowers.

This cheetah is running fast, but it cannot catch the birds.

26

One eagle has some food, but the other eagle wants it.

27

1 Animals are always hungry.   F

2 It is not easy to find food.   ....

3 Some animals want food from flowers.   ....

4 All animals can run very fast.   ....

5 All animals want the same food.   ....

Level 2

The Gingerbread Man	**Sly Fox and Red Hen**	**The Monster Next Door**	**Wild Animals**	**Little Red Riding Hood**
978-0-241-25442-4	978-0-241-25443-1	978-0-241-25444-8	978-0-241-25445-5	978-0-241-25446-2
Dinosaurs	**Topsy and Tim The Big Race**	**Goes to the Treehouse**	**Sports Day**	**Going on a Picnic**
978-0-241-25447-9	978-0-241-25448-6	978-0-241-25449-3	978-0-241-26222-1	978-0-241-26221-4
Peter Rabbit and the Angry Owl	**Superhero Max**	**We Can Help!**	**Daddy Pig's New Van**	**School Trip**
978-0-241-28369-1	978-0-241-28368-4	978-0-241-28367-7	978-0-241-28371-4	978-0-241-28372-1
The Peter Rabbit Club	**Daddy Pig's Office**	**Spring is Here!**	**Great Trains**	**Hungry Animals**
978-0-241-29811-4	978-0-241-29814-5	978-0-241-29809-1	978-0-241-29808-4	978-0-241-29844-2

Now you're ready for Level 3!